A Handbook for

Citizen Farmers
Plant every seed in your life with love.

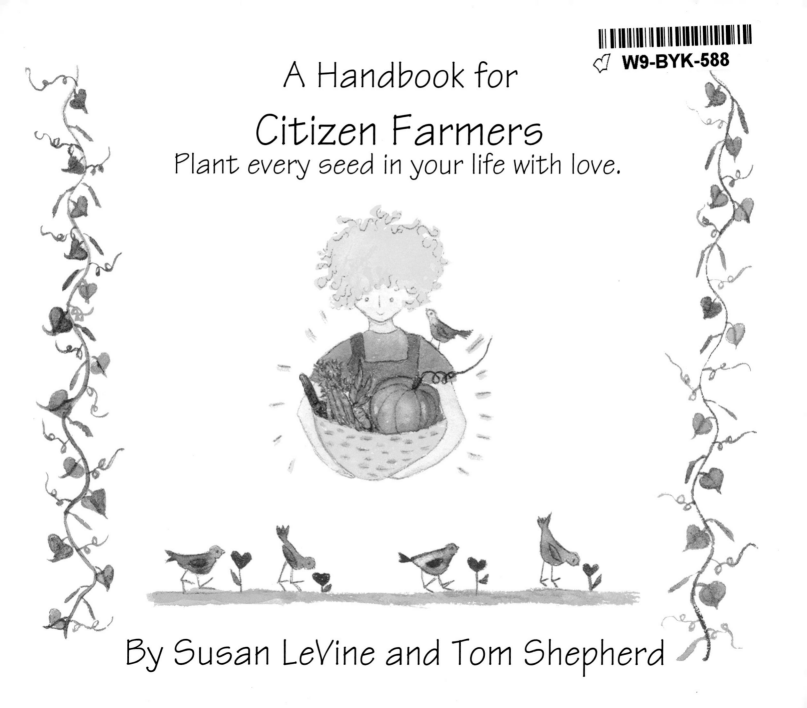

By Susan LeVine and Tom Shepherd

Dedication

We dedicate this book to Alice Waters for educating so many children about growing gardens that nurture themselves and their loved ones.
Also, we dedicate this book to all of the children who touch our lives and have inspired us to write this book.

1. Selecting Your Garden Site

Veggies, for instance, like full sun so make sure that you pick a happy home for them to grow in.

2. Preparing The Soil

Remove the existing weeds. Turn the soil with the shovel. Break up the dirt clods and add organic material such as compost.

3. Planting The Seeds

The larger the seed, the deeper you plant. Small seeds like carrots and lettuce are planted very shallow - only 1/4" below the surface. Large seeds, like beans, are planted deeper. Soil moisture should be not too wet and not too dry. Seeds need some moisture but seeds don't like muddy homes to grow in.

4. When a Seed Sprouts, it is Called Germination

All seeds germinate at different rates or speeds. All seeds have different seasons. Most seeds germinate (or sprout) in one to two weeks. Whispering "I love you" to your seeds help them to grow.

5. Protecting Your Little Sprouts (otherwise called seedlings)

When the seed breaks the ground and becomes a seedling it is vulnerable, which means it is open to be eaten by critters, such as squirrels, snails, and birds. Do what you can to protect your seedlings. Things like strawberry baskets let in the needed sun but keep the critters away.

6. Watering Schedule

Your watering time must change if it rains or if it is too hot. It is important to water deeply so that plants will develop a deep root system.

7. Staking Your Plants

Some plants need to be staked and strung, such as tomatoes, peas and some green beans.

8. Cultivating (Breaking up the Soil)

It is important that the ground around your plants be weed-free and loose. Use a hoe to break up the soil as this helps the water to penetrate to the root zone.

9. Harvesting

Different plants have a different time to be picked. They will tell you when they are ready.

10. Enjoy Eating Your Harvest with Friends and Family

It feels good to help your loved ones eat healthy.

Eats You Can Grow...

Tomatoes

Cucumbers

Melons

Strawberries

Green Beans

...In Your Garden

Squash

Carrots

Peppers

Salad Greens

Carrots

Carrots are a small seed and are planted very shallow(about 1/4"). You can plant carrots close together (1/4" apart). The soil must be moist (not muddy) until you see the seed germinating and braking thru the soil, then water less. After two months, you can start harvesting baby carrots. Carrots can continue to be harvested for a long period.

Squash

Squash are large seeds and are planted deep (1-2"). Plant about 6" apart. Once the seeds have emerged (germinated), thin plants so that eventually the plants will be two feet apart.

Salad Greens

Salad greens come from very small seeds. Plant 1/4" deep. The seed emerges (germinates) in one week! Keep the soil moist until the seed emerges and plant the seeds very close together: about 2" apart. Then when the greens emerge, thin them so they are not over-crowded.

Melons

Melons come from a medium-size seed and are planted an inch deep. You only want a couple of plants in your garden as they take up a large space. They must be planted at the early part of the summer to get a good melon.

Strawberries

Strawberries are best started in your garden from little plants that you buy in the nursery. Plant so the roots are straight down in the ground with the crown of the plant level with the soil surface. Plant 8" apart.

Cucumbers

Cucumbers start with a medium seed and are planted about 1" deep. When the seed germinates (when the plant emerges), thin (or remove extra plants) to be 4" apart. First you will see flowers, then look for cucumbers.

Tomatoes

Buy plants from the nursery instead of growing from a seed. When planting your tomato plant, plant deeply at the level of the first leaf on the stem of the plant. Two favorite varieties are Early Girls and Brandy Wines. Both of these varieties need staking and should be planted three feet apart.

Green Beans

Green beans come from a large seed and should be planted 2" deep. Plant seeds 1" apart. Water one time until you see the plant emerge (or germinate). Beans are very sensitive to overwatering. No thinning necessary. In approximately two months, flowers will bloom and soon after beans will appear. Pick beans when they are young and tender.

Peppers

Peppers are a long season crop and are best started from seedlings. Set plants about 1 foot apart in rows. Plant when all danger of frost has past.

Seed Varieties

For each type of vegetable, there are many varieties. We have selected our favorite varieties to teach you how to grow. Seeds are available at www.citizenfarmer.org

About the Authors

Tom Shepherd has been an organic farmer since 1973 in the Santa Barbara, California area. Tom grows vegetables and herbs, fruit trees and table grapes. He teaches about organic farming to area school children and students at UCSB. He provides food to local residents through farmers markets, CSAs, restaurants and for the local school program. Tom invented many solar machines that make farming easy, like his solar salad spinner. Tom is passionate about growing organically and about the benefits of eating organically. He is a true artist in the field and anyone who eats one of his strawberries knows this.

Susan LeVine is an accomplished writer and artist. She has been a licensed artist for Recycled Paper Greetings since 1998 and has illustrated book covers and other things. Susan is most known for her company, Uccellino, a company that sells inspirational products like Guide Birds, Spheres of Wonder and Message boxes. Susan is a passionate bird lover and paints birds and sells them in local Santa Barbara galleries as well as a plein aire artist. Susan is happy to have had the opportunity to collaborate with Tom and make his dream of creating a book to inspire children to grow things a reality.